MLA guidelines

9TH EDITION

- This is a guide to **Modern Language Association (MLA)** rules used in academic writing
- **Important:** The rules covered in this guide are accurate according to the *MLA Handbook* 9th edition

What Is MLA Style?

- A set of guidelines, also known as an **editorial style,** developed by the Modern Language Association (MLA) for use in the humanities
- Establishes trust via citations in text that refer to a works cited list
- Has been in use by students and scholars since 1951 and is based on the consensus of scholars in language, literature, and other fields in the humanities
- Provides a template for documentation through essential pieces of information that almost all sources have, including:
  - Title, Author, Publication date
- These essential elements allow writers to assess source validity and uniformly cite all types of work

Research & Writing

- The research paper is a form of **exploration** and **communication**
  - **Exploration:** Research requires writers to explore subjects through **primary research** (first-hand investigation) and **secondary research** (the examination of other researchers' work)
  - **Communication:** A research paper should present ideas in a concise manner through thorough research and effective writing mechanics
- When selecting research topics, be specific, consult other sources before finalizing the topic, and revise the topic if necessary
- Use outlines (working to final outlines) and drafts (first to final drafts) in order to create the best possible research paper

Finding & Using Sources

- Use a combination of sources, but an academic library with professional reference librarians and electronic databases will likely be the most reliable resource
- To initiate research, use reference works
- Reference works categorize and contribute data that aid in the location of sources

NOTE: Reference works are meant to initiate research and aid in finding sources; some reference works may not be used in the paper itself and may instead direct researchers to more appropriate sources

Reference Works

- Reference works are a useful way to locate new information and provide a concise method for evaluating numerous sources quickly
- Reference works include:
  - **Indexes:** Alphabetical subject lists used to locate material in newspapers, journals, magazines, and writings in book collections
    EX: *The New York Times Article Archives, Readers' Guide to Periodical Literature, General Science Index, Education Index*
  - **Bibliographies:** Lists of related materials and publications
    EX: *Bibliographic Index, MLA International Bibliography*

- **Abstract collections:** Summaries of journal articles
  EX: *Sociological Abstracts, Dissertation Abstracts International, Physics Abstracts, Historical Abstracts*
- **Research guides:** Concise sources of information and scholarly works related to many areas of study
  EX: *Literary Research Guide; Guide to Reference Books; Nursing Research: Methods, Critical Appraisal, and Utilization*
- **Dictionaries:** Alphabetical listings that cover a variety of words and topics from the general to the very specific
  EX: *Merriam-Webster's Dictionary, The Oxford English Dictionary, The Interpreter's Dictionary of the Bible, Taber's Cyclopedic Medical Dictionary, Black's Law Dictionary*
- **Encyclopedias:** Alphabetical collections containing information on a variety of subjects
  EX: *The New Encyclopaedia Britannica, The Film Encyclopedia, The Visual Encyclopedia of Science*
- **Biographical sources:** Information on living and deceased persons
  EX: *Who's Who in America, Current Biography, Merriam-Webster's Biographical Dictionary*
- **Atlases:** Collections of maps
  EX: *The Times Atlas of the World, Geographica: The Complete Illustrated Atlas of the World*
- Many publishers release both **print** and **electronic versions** of a work; the electronic version may be a website, a digital file, or a database of information
- Searching reference databases
  - **Author searches:** Enter the name of a scholar to produce a list of titles by the author
  - **Title searches:** Enter the title of a work to find the bibliographic information contained in the database; this can also recall titles of works based on a partial title search (e.g., "A Tale of Two")
  - **Subject searches:** Enter a phrase or term that describes the subject matter (e.g., "horror fiction") to produce a list of works
  - **Boolean searches:** Use searches based on Boolean logic with the operators *and, or,* and *not* (e.g., "A Christmas Carol NOT Charles Dickens" for all titles with that name not written by Dickens)

Working Bibliographies

- A working bibliography is a list of sources that grows and changes as research is conducted
- Document all publication information in a working bibliography to avoid accidental plagiarism later in the paper
- Working bibliographies can be outlined or arranged as needed by the researcher to show connections between works and to better aid in organization; however, once the bibliography has been turned into a works cited page, it must be alphabetized and cited appropriately

NOTE: Working bibliographies are ***not* works cited** lists; they include notes along with important publication information, which will then be used when citing the documents

Source Evaluation

- As there are many types of sources available to researchers, the MLA recommends careful evaluation of sources before using them
- Sources should be evaluated based on verifiability, accuracy, publication date, and publication status
  - **Peer-reviewed articles,** which are evaluated by professionals in the field before publication, are the ideal source due to a stringent publishing process
  - **Internet sources** must be carefully evaluated to ensure accuracy and verifiability; to assess Internet sources, confirm that the website has:
    - An **author,** preferably with provided credentials
    EX: Gwendolyn Wright, State University
    - **Sponsorship** from a reputable organization, as stated in its access information (e.g., .edu, .org, .gov)
    EX: The University of Colorado, Central Intelligence Agency
    - **Editor** information and an editorial policy
    EX: Each contributor and article is reviewed by general editors Stephen DeFoe, Malcolm Ginsburg, and Nicholas Winters.
- When evaluating Internet sources, check the sponsoring organization to ensure that the page is not an advertisement
- **Self-published** books and websites should be evaluated to confirm factual accuracy

Plagiarism & Academic Integrity

- **What is plagiarism?**
  - The MLA defines plagiarism as using someone else's work or ideas as your own
  - Plagiarism can be intentional or unintentional, but it is always unethical
- **Consequences of plagiarism**
  - The academic penalty for plagiarism varies depending on institution; in the professional world, it may result in the loss of a job and credibility
    - Plagiarism can destroy public trust in an entire field, as well as financially and ethically impacting those whose work was stolen
    - **Unintentional plagiarism is often caused by:**
    - Not understanding the concept of plagiarism
  - Poor research and note-taking habits, particularly when personal notes and source notes become mixed
  - Copying text word-for-word without using quotation marks or proper documentation, even if a citation is included
  - Copying an author's sentence structure for the sake of grammatical accuracy

Forms of Plagiarism

Repeating or paraphrasing wording without proper documentation

Source:
This first stage of the mythological journey—which we have designated the "call to adventure"—signifies that destiny has summoned the hero and transferred his spiritual center of gravity from within the pale of his society to a zone unknown.
Campbell, Joseph. *The Hero with a Thousand Faces*. Novato, CA: New World Library, 2008. Print.

Plagiarism:
A hero must first receive—and subsequently deny—a call to adventure in order to fulfill his or her destiny.

Proper Presentation:
As Joseph Campbell explains in his seminal work, *The Hero with a Thousand Faces*, the hero must first be called to action in order to fulfill his future destiny (48).

Using a particularly apt phrase from an original source without documentation

Plagiarism:
When a hero enters the threshold, the belly of the whale, he or she must conquer the power within.

Proper Presentation:
When a hero enters the threshold, "the belly of the whale," he or she must conquer the power within (Campbell 74).

Paraphrasing an argument or a line of thinking without proper documentation

Source:
It would not be too much to say that myth is the secret opening through which the inexhaustible energies of the cosmos pour into the human cultural manifestation.

　Campbell, Joseph. *The Hero with a Thousand Faces*. Novato, CA: New World Library, 2008. Print.

Plagiarism:
Myth is the lens through which humans understand the universe and themselves.

Proper Presentation:
Joseph Campbell describes myth as the "secret opening" that allows mankind to relate universal "energies" to cultural manifestations, such as religion, philosophies and science (1). In other words, myth becomes the lens through which humans comprehend the universe and themselves.

- Documentation is not needed when an idea is either broadly known by the readers or widely accepted by scholars (e.g., historic dates or biographical information)
  EX: William Shakespeare was an English playwright whose plays are still performed today.
- Purchasing papers is also considered plagiarism, as the ideas within the paper are not that of the author
- Reusing prior research and papers is plagiarism, as this has already received academic credit
- Collaborative papers require each contributor to receive credit for their work

You do not need to cite: allusions to rhetorically common phrases (e.g., we used the Force), common knowledge, epigraphs, and passing mentions

Research Paper Format

- Type and print text on one side of standard 8.5 × 11-inch paper
- Double-space text for the entire paper, including the title
- Use 12-point font size in a consistent, legible typeface
- Justify left and set all margins to one inch
- Do **not** create a title page
- On the first page, before beginning the paper, type your name, the instructor's name, course number, and date separated by double-spaced lines
- The title of the paper should be centered and double-spaced with one line separating it from the text
- Create a header and number the pages in the upper right-hand corner
  - The header should include last name and page number
  - The header should be one-half inch from the top and flush with the right margin
- Keep any internal headings and subheadings consistent
  - Headings should be left-justified and not indented
  - Do **not** include heading levels if there is only one instance of this level
- Place tables, illustrations, and lists in text, as close to textual references as possible
  - Lists should be integrated into text as often as possible; if not, vertical lists may be stylized as complete sentences with standard punctuation, bulleted with no punctuation, or separated by semicolons and concluded with a period
- Include any endnotes on a separate page before the list of works cited
  - Endnotes are used to avoid long, explanatory notes in the body of the text
  - The notes page should be titled *Notes* (centered, do **not** bold, italicize, or underline; use *Note* if there is only one note)
  - Notes should be double-spaced and listed by consecutive Arabic numbers that correspond to the notation in text
  - Place a period and a space after each endnote number
  - Notes should be indented five spaces; subsequent lines in a note should be flush with the left margin

Inclusive Language Principles

- **Inclusive language** allows writers to reach and recognize audience intersectionality; context and audience should be considered when making language choices
- **Relevance**
  - Make sure references to identity are relevant or necessary for context
    - Ask questions such as: Does the audience need to know this person's gender? Do they need to know their religious background? Is this description making the subject appear outside of normal assumptions and is that necessary?
- **Gender-specific language**
  - Use gender-neutral language as often as possible to avoid audience exclusion
    EX: *mankind* can be switched to *humankind*
  - Avoid gendered terms that refer to populations or occupations unless relevant
    EX: *Latino* or *Latina* can be *Latinx*
    EX: *policeman* can be *police officer*
- **Pronouns**
  - Minimize use of pronouns that refer to gender or sex unless relevant to the research
    - Non-gender-specific pronouns such as *they/their* can refer to individuals
    - Using both or alternating between female and male pronouns is also acceptable, but eliminating gendered pronouns is preferable unless relevant
  - Do **not** assume pronouns; use *they/their* if preferred pronouns are not known
  - Do **not** assume audience identity
    - Use *we/our* sparingly as this assumes the audience identifies with the writer
- **People-first & identity-first language**
  - Choosing terms that do not negatively judge or define a subject by one aspect of their experience is known as **people-first language**
    EX: a person with vision loss, a person on parole
  - Do **not** use language that implies feeling or evokes images about an identity
    EX: A person is not "suffering from" or "afflicted with" a disability.
  - Alternately, **identity-first language** can be used when the subject's identity is the focus
    EX: A Gay-Straight Alliance is an organization that prefers to use identity-first language in their name.
- **Styling within text**
  - Do **not** use style that undermines the identity of groups or people
    EX: quotation marks or italics around a community or individual's identity, such as "black" instead of black
  - Capitalize appropriately; if unsure consult a community member or dictionary
    EX: black, Black, and African American are often used interchangeably, but writers should confirm and use preferred terms

Citing Sources in Text

- Quoting and paraphrasing are used to refer to the works of others
- When quoting or paraphrasing, always:
  - Try to keep quotations short and to the point; only use them when necessary
  - Provide the author's name (or the title of the work) and the page, paragraph, or line number of the work in a **parenthetical citation**
    EX: (*Author quoted but not named in text*) At the school of the Bobadilla sisters, older girls were taught how to sew, knit, crochet, and read, "but they will not learn how to write, so that even if they receive a love letter, they will not be able to write one back" (Alvarez 16).
    EX: (*Author named in text with a quote*) Joseph Campbell regards the myth as "living inspiration of whatever else may have appeared out of the activities of the human body and mind" (1).
    EX: (*Author named but not quoted in text*) Campbell's concept of the monomyth explains how the myth was created to explain human activities and relationships (1).
- **If a work has no author**, use the title of the work in place of the author's name. If the title is longer than a noun phrase, shorten it to the initial noun and any preceding adjectives, leaving out initial articles. If the title does not begin with a noun phrase, use the first word
  EX: Abbreviate *In the Name of Salome* as *Name* (*Name 3*).
  EX: Abbreviate *Natural Supernaturalism: Tradition and Revolution in Romantic Literature* as *Natural Supernaturalism* (*Natural Supernaturalism* 390).
- **For works that are written by corporate identities** (e.g., universities, government agencies), cite the corporate identity as the author (Natl. Center for Education Statistics 2)
- **If a work does not have pagination** (e.g., some websites, films, broadcasts), refer to the work in the sentence or cite the name of the work alone
  EX: Francis Ford Coppola's *Apocalypse Now* explores themes of alienation and "the other," particularly in Kurtz's final words of "the horror; the horror."
  EX: Kurtz's "horror" during the climax reinforces themes of alienation and "the other" (*Apocalypse Now*).
  - **If the work contains other identifying information** (e.g., a novel or play), include the abbreviation before the number (Chan, par. 41)
  - **To include other part references along with a page number**, use a semicolon after the page number (Miller 9; act 1) or (185; ch. 13, sec. 2)
- **Many medieval works** and ancient Greek and Roman works are referenced by the page number followed by the part number
  EX: "1453a15–16" to refer to page 1453, left-hand column (a), lines 15–16
- **If referencing an entire work**, do **not** include page numbers but do include the work in the works cited list
  EX: The concept of the monomyth as detailed in *The Hero with a Thousand Faces* functions as a guide for comparative studies in mythology.
- **If referencing multiple sources in the same parenthetical citation**, separate the sources with semicolons (Baron 194; Jacobs 55)
- **If referencing different locations in a single source in the same parenthetical citation**, separate the page numbers with commas (Baron 194, 200)
- **If referencing multiple works by the same author**, include the title of the work in the citation (King, *On Writing* 101)
- **To reference two works by the same author in the same parenthetical citation**, separate the titles by *and* (Gluck, "Ersatz Thought" and "For"); otherwise, use commas and *and* (Gluck, "Ersatz Thought," "For," and Foreword)
- **If two authors share the same last name**, use the author's first initial in the citation to clarify (P. Wright 145)
- **If referencing altered quotations**, separate the explanation from the citation with a semicolon (Baron 194; my emphasis) or (29; 1st ellipsis in original)
- **If referencing a non-English source**, the citation may begin with the translation followed by the sources of the two versions separated by semicolons
  EX: At the opening of Dante's *Inferno*, the poet finds himself in "una selva oscura" ("a dark wood"; 1.2; Ciardi 28).
- **If quoting or citing from an indirect source**, document the source as **quoted in** with the abbreviation *qtd. in* as part of the parenthetical citation
  EX: Shelley described the decades preceding the French Revolution as "an age of despair" (qtd. in Abrams 328).
- If a parenthetical citation falls in the same place as other parenthetical content, combine the two by placing the more immediately relevant one first and enclosing the second in square brackets
- Provide full citation information for the work in your works cited list
- All parenthetical references included in text must match the corresponding information in your list of works cited

Works Cited

Abrams, M. H. *Natural Supernaturalism: Tradition and Revolution in Romantic Literature*. Norton, 1973.

Alvarez, Julia. *In the Name of Salome*. Algonquin Books, 2000.

Apocalypse Now. Directed by Francis Ford Coppola, performed by Martin Sheen and Marlon Brando, Paramount, 2001.

Campbell, Joseph. *The Hero with a Thousand Faces*. New World Library, 2008.

King, Stephen. *On Writing: A Memoir of the Craft*. Scribner, 2010.

Titles of Works

- Capitalize the first word, final word, all principal words, and all nouns, pronouns, subordinating conjunctions, verbs, adverbs, and adjectives
  EX: *The Little Prince, One Flew Over the Cuckoo's Nest, To Kill a Mockingbird*
- Do **not** capitalize articles, prepositions, coordinating conjunctions, or the infinitive *to* unless these are used to start a subtitle
- For titles in languages other than English, capitalize the first word and all regularly capitalized words in that language
- Italicize titles of works that are independent, such as a book; play; collection of essays, stories, or poems; title of a periodical; title of a tv series; website; etc.
- Place titles of works that are part of a larger work in quotation marks, such as an article, essay, chapter, story, poem, episode in a tv series, posting or article on a website, song on an album, etc.
  EX: "The Shoemaker" from Dickens' *A Tale of Two Cities*
- When referencing a title within the title of a work, italicize or use quotations as normally referenced
  EX: Journal Article: "*A Tale of Two Cities* and Social Injustice in the Victorian Era"
  EX: Essay about a poem: "Emotions after Hearing 'Crossing Brooklyn Ferry'"
- Do **not** italicize or use quotation marks when referencing scriptural writings; political documents; or conferences, workshops, and courses. Only italicize scriptural writings if they are in an individually published edition, which can be cited as any other published book
  EX: Many passages from the Bible explore the relationship of humans to one another.
  EX: *The Bible: The Authorized King James Version* features edits that adhere to the Church of England's belief system.
- If a poem or short message is untitled, use the first line as the title exactly as it appears
  EX: The tweet "Potatoes wish they could be our fries when they grow up" by Wendy's (@wendys) shows how the restaurant chain has turned to informal messaging via social media to connect with consumers.
- If titles are frequently used in a paper, they may be shortened after initial introduction
  EX: *Dr. Strangelove or: How I Learned to Stop Worrying and Love the Bomb* can be shortened to *Dr. Strangelove*.
- For variations of style in cases such as serial commas, question marks, exclamation points, or colons, use the title or publishing authority's style when referring to the work

Quotations

- Choose quotations carefully and do **not** overuse them
- Keep quotations as brief as possible in order to maintain reader interest
- Introduce quotations using accurate sentence structure to ensure clarity in writing
  - Quotations can be directly integrated into writing
    EX: After heroes answer the call, their first initiation into the journey is to encounter "a protective figure (often a little old crone or old man) who provides the adventurer with amulets against the dragon forces he is about to pass" (Campbell 57).
  - Quotations can be introduced
    EX: As Joseph Campbell states, "For those who have not refused the call, the first encounter of the hero-journey is with a protective figure (often a little old crone or old man) who provides the adventurer with amulets against the dragon forces he is about to pass" (57).
  - Quotations can be placed anywhere in a sentence, including the middle
    EX: A hero may need "amulets against the dragon forces he is about to pass" if he intends to succeed on his journey (Campbell 57).
- Use ellipses to show omissions or incompletions in the quote; do **not** omit text if it changes context or meaning
  EX: Campbell states that a hero will need, "a protective figure…who provides the adventurer with amulets against the dragon forces he is about to pass" (57).
- If a quotation is longer than four lines, it must be shown as a block quotation without quotation marks
  - Use a colon to introduce the quote
  - Do **not** use quotation marks
  - Indent one inch from the left margin
  - Double-space the block quote
  - Following the paragraph, use a parenthetical citation set off from the text, with no period following the citation
    EX: The first paragraph of *A Tale of Two Cities* introduces the vast differences between Paris and London during the French Revolution:

  > It was the best of times, it was the worst of times, it was the age of wisdom, it was the age of foolishness, it was the epoch of belief, it was the epoch of incredulity, it was the season of Light, it was the season of Darkness, it was the spring of hope, it was the winter of despair, we had everything before us, we had nothing before us, we were all going direct to Heaven, we were all going direct the other way—in short, the period was so far like the present period, that some of its noisiest authorities insisted on its being received, for good or for evil, in the superlative degree of comparison only. (Dickens 1)

  Dickens, Charles. "A Tale of Two Cities." *Google Books*. James Nisbet & Company, 1908. Web. 28 Jan. 2015.

- To quote poetry, do **not** cite the page number; cite the poem line number instead
  - Incorporate single lines as regular quotations and two to three lines in a regular quotation with a slash indicating the line break
    EX: Whitman describes the transcendental nature of his ferry ride in "Crossing Brooklyn Ferry" with the phrasing: "It avails not, time nor place—distance avails not" (20).
    EX: In "Crossing Brooklyn Ferry," Whitman describes his ferry ride as a transcendental experience, stating: "It avails not, time nor place—distance avails not, / I am with you, you men and women of a generation or / ever so many generations hence" (20–22).
  - For verse quotations, begin on a new line and indent one inch from the left margin; cite the line numbers in a parenthetical citation set off from the text without a period
    EX: Whitman uses detailed imagery to show his view from the ferry:

  > Ah, what can ever be more stately and admirable to me than mast-hemm'd Manhattan?
  > River and sunset and scallop-edg'd waves of flood-tide?
  > The sea-gulls oscillating their bodies, the hay-boat in the twilight, and the belated lighter? (93–97)

  Whitman, Walt, and Francis Murphy. "Crossing Brooklyn Ferry." *The Complete Poems*. Harmondsworth, Middlesex: Penguin, 1986. 189–96. Print.

- When quoting dialogue from a play, use the same block quote conventions to set the dialogue apart from the text
  - Indent one inch from the left side
  - All subsequent lines in the same character's speech should be indented an additional quarter of an inch
  - Begin each line with the character's name, in capital letters, followed by a period
  - Include all stage directions as stated exactly in the text
  - As with poetry, cite the lines from the play in a parenthetical citation following the final sentence, with no period or punctuation following the citation
    EX: Miranda's inexperience and naiveté is expressed through *The Tempest*'s most famous lines as she views the crowd of shipwrecked humans:

  > MIRANDA. O, wonder!
  >   How many goodly creatures are there here!
  >   How beauteous mankind is! O brave new world,
  >   That has such people in't!
  > PROSPERO. 'Tis new to thee. (203–207)

  Shakespeare, William. *The Tempest*. Mineola, NY: Dover Publications, 1999. Print.

- When quoting a translation or translating directly for the reader, include the translation and the source, if there is one, in parentheticals following the translation

Works Cited

- The works cited page appears at the end of the paper
- Begin the list on a new page and double-space it
- Title the page *Works Cited*
  - If only one source is used in the paper, title the page *Work Cited*
  - If you include works you consult but do not borrow from in this list, title the page *Works Consulted*; for a combination, use *Works Cited and Consulted*
- The title should be centered an inch from the top of the page; do **not** bold, italicize, or underline
- Each entry should be left-justified, and if subsequent lines are needed for an entry, they should be indented one-half inch (five spaces)

The Core Elements

- **Author**
  - List the author's last name, a comma, the rest of the name as it appears in the work, and then a period unless the name already ends with a period
  - List entries alphabetically by the author's last name
  - List and alphabetize pseudonyms, online handles, names without surnames, and corporate authors as they appear in the work; if online handles have an author name attached, refer to standard author conventions and use brackets to show username (Martin, George RR [@GRRMspeaking])
  - If an author uses a surname before a given name, common in Asian languages such as Japanese or Vietnamese, do **not** include a comma (Duong Thu Huong)
  - If a work has two authors, order them as they appear in the work. List the first author with the last name first, insert a comma and *and*, followed by the second name in normal order (Bernecker, Sven, and Fred Dretske)
  - If a work has three or more authors, list the first author with the last name first, a comma, and *et al.*, which is italicized (George, Michael L., *et al.*)
  - If the author(s) is anyone other than the creator of the main work (edited collections documented as a whole, translated works if the focus is on the translation, films or tv series with the focus on a particular person), insert a comma and the person's role after their name. Put the creator of the main work where **other contributors** would go (By Fyodor Dostoevsky)
  - If two or more entries by two authors begin with the same name, alphabetize by the last names of the second authors listed
  - For more than one work by a single author, including corporate authors, list the entries alphabetically by title and use three hyphens (---) in place of the author's name in the second and subsequent entries, followed by a period
- **Title of source**
  - List the title, any subtitle (*see* **Mechanics of Writing**), and a period
  - If the author's name is unknown; if the author of the work is the organization that published it; or if the work is a film, tv show, or other work without a focus on one particular person, alphabetize by title (ignoring any initial *A*, *An*, or *The*)

- When using long introductory phrases or clauses
  EX: While the use of hydrocarbons in manufacturing and mechanical production is well recognized, their use in other fields may come as a surprise.
- When setting off alternative or contrasting phrases
  EX: In this murder mystery it was the mother-in-law's third cousin, not the butler, who did it.
- When words, phrases, or clauses act as a series
  EX: The correct use of the Oxford comma has been debated by writers, scholars, and journalists for decades.
- When presenting dates in the month/day/year style, but not the day/month/year style, or when a month and a year or a season and a year are written
  EX: The first Bloomsday took place on June 16, 1094 in James Joyce's *Ulysses*; I plan to attend in spring 2022.
- When writing a location as a place-name
  EX: The town of Nederland, Colorado has a yearly festival celebrating a cryogenically frozen man.
- When setting off nonrestrictive clauses beginning with *who, whom, whose, which,* or *that*
  EX: Kathryn, who works as a rodeo clown, is also a prima ballerina.
- When using a short clause to introduce a sentence, a comma is optional, but use should remain consistent throughout the writing
  EX: Every winter, deciduous trees go dormant and draw on stored nutrients to survive. *OR*
  Every winter deciduous trees go dormant and draw on stored nutrients to survive.
- When using specific phrases like *therefore, of course, perhaps,* and *indeed,* commas are optional when not joining two independent clauses
  EX: Walt Whitman was born in New York and his work, indeed, expresses a love for the city. *OR*
  Walt Whitman was indeed born in New York, and his work expresses a love for the city.

• A **semicolon** acts as a link
- Between independent clauses if they are not linked by a conjunction
  EX: The manuscript is flawed beyond belief; still, Jack thinks he can rewrite it before the deadline.
- Between items in a series when the items contain commas
  EX: Seated around the table were Uncle Frank, the henpecked husband; Aunt Matilda, the know-it-all; Cousin Pete, the bore; and me, the only normal one at the family reunion.

• A **colon** has many uses
- Before the second part of a sentence to elaborate on the first part
  EX: Even after practicing for months, Steve only placed third at the swim meet: During the race, he couldn't see because his goggles kept filling up with water.
- To introduce a list
  EX: There were three unusual books on the reading list: *Infinite, Long Night of the Moon,* and *Kachina.*
- To introduce a rule or principle; in this case, use a capital letter after the colon
  EX: Author Thomas F. Monteleone has one hard, fast rule for success: A writer writes.
- To introduce a quotation that is independent of the sentence itself
  EX: In Robert Morgan's book, *The Truest Pleasure,* Ginny is bewildered when she sees a meteor streak through the sky for the first time: "Lord help us. Is this the Rapture?"

• **Hyphens** are used to connect terms and phrases
- Add a hyphen when creating a compound adjective, typically when using an adverb and noun combination to describe another noun
  EX: well-dressed businessman, off-campus housing, on-site laundry, better-informed citizens
- Do **not** hyphenate when a compound adjective follows a noun
  EX: The apartment was off campus.
- Do **not** hyphenate compound adjectives that use adverbs with an *-ly* ending or *too, very,* or *much*
  EX: nicely written paper, wonderfully explained research, much hated politician, a too aggressive comedian
- Hyphenate ages and time periods unless they are pluralized
  EX: We have a three-year-old shih tzu. *OR*
  Our shih tzu is three years old.
- Add a hyphen when using an adjective to describe a compound adjective
  EX: The shih tzu is a descendant of late-fifteenth-century dogs owned by monks in Tibet.
- Hyphenate compound adjectives that are formed from a number
  EX: twenty-year mortgage, ten-day fast, sixteen-week semester
- Hyphenate all compound numbers when written out, from twenty-one through ninety-nine
- Hyphenate nouns that are equal to one another
  EX: writer-editor, singer-songwriter
- Do **not** hyphenate noun groups in which the first noun acts as a modifier
  EX: dog lover, soccer player, horror writer
- Do **not** hyphenate prefixes (e.g., *multi, post, pre, un*) unless the hyphen clarifies spelling issues with the prefix or is used before a capital letter
  EX: postwar, multilingual, overdraft, postmodern, antebellum Pseudo-Elizabethan, post-World War I, post-traumatic, de-icing, re-sign

NOTE: In the second example, *re-sign* is hyphenated to clarify that it is not the word *resign* but instead signifies signing something again

• An **apostrophe** is used to show possession or create a contraction
- Add an apostrophe and an *s* to form the possessive of a singular noun
  EX: the guitar's strings, the president's commission, the town's charter
- Add an apostrophe after the *s* to form the possessive of a plural noun
  EX: the teachers' books, the visitors' passes, the consultants' ideas, the scouts' campfires
- In the case of singular nouns in a series, use a single apostrophe and an *s*
  EX: Billy, Tommy, and Linda's dog; Smith and Southworth's book
- Add an apostrophe to form the possessive of a plural proper noun
  EX: the Kennedys' complex, the Vanderbilts' enterprises, the Grants' library cards
- Add an apostrophe to pluralize letters
  EX: straight A's, catch some z's
- Do **not** use an apostrophe to form the plural form of an abbreviation or a number
  EX: DVDs, 1700s, VCRs, MP3s, CDs, MDs, 7s
- Do **not** use an apostrophe to form a possessive version of the pronoun *it*, as an apostrophe indicates a contraction of *it is*
  EX: My manuscript has a mind of its own; I swear, it's erasing my progress every night when I go to sleep.

NOTE: Contractions (e.g., *can't, aren't, wouldn't, didn't*) are seldom used in academic writing

• **Dashes** and **parentheses** are used to show a sharp break in sentence continuity
- Use to set apart an element that would otherwise interrupt the sentence or train of thought
  EX: David picked up the bat—his father made it for him the week before—and headed toward home plate. *OR*
  David picked up the bat (his father made it for him the week before) and headed toward home plate.
- Use to set apart ideas that could be misunderstood if set apart with commas
  EX: Batman's very costume—cowl, cape, pointed ears, and bat-like wings—is designed to terrorize criminals. *OR*
  Batman's very costume (cowl, cape, pointed ears, and bat-like wings) is designed to terrorize criminals.
- A dash can also be used to introduce a list or to elaborate on what was just said

• **Slashes** should **not** be used often in formal writing and should only be used when there is no better way to express or pair opposites and relationships
  EX: (*Good*) Milton's "Paradise Lost" is a fundamental example of good/evil representations in an epic poem.
  (*Better*) Milton's "Paradise Lost" shows the juxtaposition between good and evil through epic poetry.

• **Quotation marks** are used to set apart phrases or direct citations from writing
- When quoting directly from a source, use quotations to separate the source's phrasing from the paper itself
- Use quotation marks when inserting a phrase that is used sarcastically or to designate a particular phrasing that is idiomatic or specially used, including intentional misuse
  EX: The monster's "eyes" were no more than pale markings on its grotesque face, making us think we'd been spotted until it yawned and hunkered back down to sleep.
- When inserting a literal translation of a foreign phrase or words, quote the phrase to clearly set it apart from the text, or use single quotation marks in text to translate directly
  EX: Julius Caesar's alleged final words that signify betrayal, *et tu Brute* ("you too, Brutus?"), are often the subject of historical debate.
  EX: The word astronaut is directly derived from the Greek words *ástron*, 'star,' and *nautes*, which means sailor.

• **Periods**, **question marks**, and **exclamation points** are end punctuation marks
- Periods are used to end declarative sentences
  ▪ Do **not** add two spaces after periods or sentence endings unless instructed to do so
- Do **not** use exclamation points, except in the case of a direct quote
- Question marks end interrogative sentences; the question mark goes **inside** quotation marks if the quoted passage is a question
  EX: The client asked his lawyer, "Aren't you even going to prepare a brief?"
  ▪ Place the question mark **outside** quotation marks if the quotation is part of an overall question
  EX: When did Wordsworth write "Poem to Coleridge"?

Spelling

• Use one dictionary and choose the first-listed spelling
• Ensure that all words are spelled consistently except when using quotations
  EX: Dickens' colorless world is expressive of the social injustices in Victorian England. Even the voices of the impoverished are uncolored and pale, as seen in the shoemaker, who is described as having a voice "like a once beautiful colour faded away into a poor weak stain" (Dickens 46).

Dickens, Charles. *A Tale of Two Cities.* James Nisbet & Company, 1908. Web. 28 Jan. 2015.

• If there is a spelling or grammatical error within a direct quotation, use the Latin word *sic* in italics, enclosed in brackets, to signify the spelling error
  EX: According to the lawyer, "the client demonstrated full culpability [*sic*] for the crime."
• Do **not** divide words between lines; turn off auto-hyphenation on word processing programs
• All foreign words must retain exact spelling, including accents, capitalization, and other symbols (e.g., tildes, umlauts, accents, ampersands)

Mechanics of Writing

- MLA style focuses on clarity through consistency via different aspects of writing, including the mechanics of writing (e.g., spelling, punctuation, and quotations)

Abbreviations

- Use in the list of works cited and in tables; do **not** abbreviate within the text of a research paper, except within parentheses
  - When abbreviating, keep these guidelines in mind:
    - Do **not** begin a sentence with a lowercase abbreviation
    - Common abbreviations, such as *etc.*, *e.g.*, and *i.e.*, should be used only in parentheses; in text, write *and so forth* (etc.), *that is* (i.e.), and *for example* (e.g.)
  - Most abbreviations that end in lowercase letters are followed by a period
    EX: ch., dept., ed., no., p., par., rev., sec., trans.
  - In text, spell out the names of countries, states, counties, provinces, territories, bodies of water, and mountains
  - Use two-letter postal codes for US states and Canadian provinces in references only (e.g., NC, PQ)
  - When writing initials, put a period and a single space after each letter
    EX: J. S. Bach, F. Paul Wilson, C. S. Lewis, Charles L. Grant

Acronyms

- Do **not** use periods after letters or spaces between letters
- If an acronym is commonly used as a word, it does not require explanation (e.g., IQ, FBI, ESP)
- A term must be written out fully the first time it is used; for any subsequent references, the acronym is acceptable
  EX: National Institutes of Health (NIH)
- If an acronym is not familiar to your readers, use an expanded abbreviation
  EX: For MLA, write Mod. Lang. Assn.
- Write the plural form of an acronym without an apostrophe
  EX: Their DVDs cost too much.

Capitalization

- **Title case:** Capitalize the first word, last word, and principal words in titles and subtitles, including those that follow a hyphen in compound terms
  - Use for titles of books and articles cited in text and in references
  - Use for major headings in your paper
- **Sentence case:** Capitalize the first word, the first word after a colon, and any proper nouns in a heading or title
  - Use for titles of most non-English works
  - Use for lower-paragraph subheadings
- **Do not capitalize the following, unless they begin a title or follow a colon:**
  - **Articles:** *a*, *an*, *the*
  - **Prepositions:** *against*, *between*, *in*, *of*, *to*
  - **Conjunctions:** *and*, *but*, *for*, *nor*, *or*, *so*, *yet*
  - **Infinitive:** *to*

Italics

- Use an italic rather than an underline or bold style in research; all italicized fonts should be legible and clearly contrast regular style
- Foreign words should be italicized in English text, unless they are common abbreviations such as *et al.*, *etc.*, *genre*, *e.g.*, and *cliché*
  EX: A *siesta*, a midafternoon nap, is common in Spanish cultures.
- Any words that are being referred to as words and letters should be italicized
  EX: Although the French word *fiancé* has been adopted into English speaking and writing, the *e* often appears without an accent.
- Do **not** use italics for emphasis unless instructed to do so
- Italicize titles of major works, including books, plays, movies, art, poems published as books, websites, and databases

Names

- Upon first introduction in the paper, state the author or subject's full name, including all hyphenations and generational suffixes; upon subsequent use, simply state the author's surname
  EX: Ernest Hemingway's famously sparse prose ushered in a new wave of American literature. Hemingway himself often discussed his writing style with critics and admirers alike.
- Do **not** use formal titles such as *Miss*, *Mrs.*, or *Dr.*
- Simplified names of famous authors are acceptable, as are pseudonyms
  EX: Petrarch is acceptable in place of the full name Francesco Petrarca.
  EX: Since Mark Twain is known under this name, do **not** cite him as Samuel Clemens.
- When describing fictional characters, use character names as the work of fiction uses them, including formal titles (e.g., *Miss Havisham*, *Dr. Faustus*)
- Write and capitalize names in languages other than English according to the conventions of that language
  - Spanish personal names often include multiple distinguishing surnames as well as prepositions
    - Do **not** capitalize Spanish *de* or use alone before a surname in text or the works cited list; Spanish *del* may be capitalized in some contexts as this can be part of a surname
      EX: Miguel de Cervantes Saavedra
      - When writing these names in the paper, refer to the author as he or she is most commonly known
        EX: Miguel de Cervantes Saavedra would be discussed as Cervantes.
    - In the works cited list, alphabetize by surnames
      EX: Garcia Marquez, Gabriel
      EX: Cervantes Saavedra, Miguel de
  - Italian names follow similar conventions to Spanish names

- Italian surnames often use prepositions (*da*, *de*, *del*, *della*, *di*, *d'*), which may be capitalized and used with surnames
    EX: Andrea De Carlo would be referred to as De Carlo.
  - Alphabetize surnames in the works cited list by the author's preferred surname
    EX: De Carlo, Andrea
  - German names are often written according to English-language conventions
    - The preposition *von* is generally not capitalized or used alone with a surname in German; however, it may sometimes be capitalized in English-language contexts
      EX: The Von Trapp family
    - Names with an umlaut should be alphabetized as though the letter with the umlaut were followed by an *e*
      EX: Adam Müller would be alphabetized as Adam Mueller.
  - French names generally retain their language conventions, with a few English-language adaptations
    - When French *de* is preceded by a first name or title (e.g., *Mme.*), it should not be used alone with a surname
      EX: Honoré de Balzac would be referred to as Balzac after the initial introduction.
    - The *de* should be kept if a surname consists of one syllable
    - Retain the *d'* preposition when the following surname begins with a vowel
    - French *du* and *des* should always be capitalized and used with surnames
    - Retain all hyphens as written in names, whether they are given or surnames
      EX: Jean-Paul Sartre
  - Latin names vary depending on gender and should be written in their most commonly accepted form, not long-form
    - Roman male names include a given name, clan name, and family name; usually individuals are referred to by their clan name or surname
      EX: Gaius Julius Caesar is known as Julius Caesar.
    - Roman female names include a clan name in feminine form and a family name, usually taken from a father's family name
      EX: Annia Galeria Faustina Minor is known as Faustina the Younger.
- Capitalize names of organizations, groups, cultural movements, and literary periods, but do **not** capitalize initial articles and do **not** capitalize generic terms like movement or school
  EX: the Stuart Restoration, Art Deco architecture, Postmodernism

Numbers

- Numbers that cannot be written out in one or two words should be written in Arabic numerals
  EX: one, five, twenty-one, one hundred, eighteen hundred, 625, 1976
- Numbers can be pluralized by adding an *s* to the numeral or by treating a written number like a noun
  EX: ones, fives, twenties, 100s, 1800s
- In the case of the recurrent use of numeric, statistical, or scientific data, use numerals with units of measurement and to describe ratios or fractions
- Hyphenate compound numbers from twenty-one to ninety-nine, compounds with a number as the first element (e.g., two-way street), and the written form of fractions
- For a numbered series, use numerals unless the number is traditionally spelled out in the dictionary
  EX: page 300, number two pencil
- If a percentage or quantity can be written in fewer than three words, use written numbers; if it exceeds three written words, use numerals with symbols
  EX: fifteen thousand euros, 38.25%
- Never use symbols with written numbers
- Do **not** begin a sentence with a numeral
  EX: (*Good*) Seventeen seventy-six is an important date in American history.
  (*Better*) An important date in American history is 1776.
- Do **not** mix numerals with written numbers
  EX: Only 10 of the 125 cats were Siamese. (**not** *ten of the 125 cats*)
- Numbers in titles of works should be written out unless appearing before an abbreviation
  EX: *The History of the Number Two Pencil: A Legend of the 20th c.*
- Express decades in either written or numeral form as long as use remains consistent
- Use lowercase letters to write out centuries
- Use numerals for describing times of day unless this time is expressed in quarter and half hours or followed by o'clock
  EX: 5:45, three o'clock
- For number ranges, give the full range for numbers up to ninety-nine, roman numerals, alphanumeric numbers, and years 1 through 999 CE
- Use the last two digits of the second numeral in cases with larger numbers and for years 1000 CE or later with the same first two digits
  EX: 1980–91, 1798–1819

Punctuation

Accurate punctuation groups words into coherent phrases and clarifies sentences and sentence structure

- **Commas** are used to create continuity
  - When joining independent clauses in a sentence (use before the conjunction)
    EX: One party introduces a bill, and the other party tells them why they are wrong.
  - Between adjectives that modify the same noun
    EX: Lionel Fenn is a brilliant, underrated writer.
  - When setting off a brief parenthetical comment or an aside (use a dash or parentheses to set off longer comments)
    EX: The play was, I'm sorry to say, as bad as the critics said it would be.

- If a source is untitled (e.g., a piece in a museum), provide a description without italics or quotation marks in place of the title; if the untitled source is connected to the title of another work, such as a comment on a forum, include the title of the article in the description (Comment on "Dark Money")
- For short untitled sources, such as a tweet, use the entire text in quotation marks in place of the title. If the source is an email, use the subject of the email in quotation marks as the title

• **Title of container**
- If the source is an essay, short story, poem, article, posting, episode, or other work available as part of a larger whole, list the title of the container, styled the same as the **title of source**, followed by a comma
- When using an online source, only the place of publication is the container, not a source that links to the publication (e.g., Google Images, Blackboard, and Canvas may link to a container but may not be the container itself)
- A work may be found in two containers, such as an article in a periodical on JSTOR, a movie produced in 1973 available on Netflix, or a book published in 2000 available as an ebook

Author. Title of source. Container 1: Title of container, Other contributors, Version, Number, Publisher, Publication date, Location. Container 2: Title of container, Other contributors, Version, Number, Publisher, Publication date, Location.

• **Other contributors**
- List the unabbreviated role of any contributors (including the creator of the main work, if not listed previously), their names, and a comma
- If a source is part of a larger whole, and the contributor did not contribute to the entire container or collection, list the contributor after the title of the source, not the container
- If a source has many contributors, list the ones that are most relevant
- Descriptions of possible contributors: Adapted by, by, directed by, edited by, illustrated by, introduction by, narrated by, performed by, translated by

• **Version**
- If the source is available in any other form, list the version followed by a comma. Abbreviate *edition*
- Descriptions of possible versions: 2nd ed., King James Version, director's cut, expanded ed., revised ed., unabridged version, updated ed., version 1.3.1

• **Number**
- If the source is a book, journal, or tv show available in a series, list the part and number followed by a comma (vol. 2, no. 1, season 6, episode 8)

• **Publisher**
- List the name of the publisher followed by a comma. If a source has more than one publisher listed, use the one primarily responsible for the work. If multiple publishers are equally responsible, separate them with a forward slash (/)
- Do **not** list the publisher if the source is a periodical; self-published work; website with the same title and publisher; or website such as JSTOR, WordPress, or YouTube that is not involved in producing the work (*see* **Title of Container**, above)

• **Publication date**
- List the date of publication as it appears in the source. Insert a comma after the date if there is a location to list, or a period if it is the end of the citation
- Date stylization may vary and may include any of the following: Year, month and year, day and month, season, time stamps, ranges of dates or years
- If the source is a book, list the date on the title page or the latest copyright date
- If the source is online and the date is different from the print date, only list the date of online publication
- If the source includes the time, such as a comment on a website, list it after the date

• **Location**
- List page numbers if the source is in a container ("p. 294" or "pp. 91–124")
- If instructor or institution requires a location for an online source, list the URL or DOI without brackets
- If the source is a DVD or media set, list the disc number (disc 3)

Books

• **Books with one author**
Middlekauff, Robert. *The Glorious Cause: The American Revolution, 1763−1789*. Revised and expanded ed., Oxford UP, 2007.

• **Books with two authors or editors**
Bernecker, Sven, and Fred Dretske, editors. *Knowledge: Readings in Contemporary Epistemology*. Oxford UP, 2000.

• **Books with three or more authors or editors**
George, Michael L., *et al. The Lean Six Sigma Pocket Toolbook*. McGraw-Hill, 2005.

• **Anthology or compilation**
Williford, Lex, and Michael Martone, editors. *The Scribner Anthology of Contemporary Short Fiction*. Simon & Schuster, 2007.

• **Work within an anthology or collection**
Ueunten, Wesley Iwao. "Rising Up from a Sea of Discontent: The 1970 Koza Uprising in U.S.-Occupied Okinawa." *Militarized Currents: Toward a Decolonized Future in Asia and the Pacific*, edited by Setsu Shigematsu and Keith L. Camacho, U of Minnesota P, 2010, pp. 91–124.

• **Translated books (with a focus on the translated work)**
Rabassa, Gregory, translator. *One Hundred Years of Solitude*. By Gabriel Garcia Marquez, Random House, 1995.

• **Translated books (if the focus is not mainly on the translated work)**
Garcia Marquez, Gabriel. *One Hundred Years of Solitude*. Translated by Gregory Rabassa. Random House, 1995.

• **Books with multiple editions**
MLA Handbook. 9th ed. Modern Language Association of America, 2021.

• **Sources dated before 1900** may be cited with the city of publication in place of the publisher

Periodicals

• **Article in a scholarly journal**
Connell, R. W., and James W. Messerschmidt. "Hegemonic Masculinity: Rethinking the Concept." *Gender and Society*, vol. 19, no. 6, 2005, pp. 829–59.

Love, Glen A. "Shakespeare's Origin of Species and Darwin's Tempest." *Configurations*, vol. 18, no. 2, 2010, pp. 121–40.

Cowdery, Lauren T. "Henry James and the "Transcendent Adventure": The Search for the Self in the Introduction to *The Tempest*." *The Henry James Review*, vol. 3, no. 2, 1982, pp. 145–53.

• **Article in scholarly journal online, with URL**
O'Carroll, John, and Chris Fleming. "The Dying of the Epic." *Anthropoetics*, vol. 16, no. 2, 2011. www.anthropoetics.ucla.edu/ap1602.

• **Article in online database, with URL**
Daft, Richard L., and Arie Y. Lewin. "Where Are the Theories for the 'New' Organizational Forms? An Editorial Essay." *Organization Science*, vol. 4, no. 4, 1993, pp. i–vi. *JSTOR*, www.jstor.org/stable/2635077.

• **Newspaper article**
Savage, David G. "Redistricting Push Puts a Lot on Line." *Sun-Sentinel* [Fort Lauderdale], 14 Aug. 2011, p. 3A.

• **Magazine article**
- Abbreviate all months with the exception of May, June, and July
- Do **not** give volume and issue numbers even if they are listed
Laurent, Olivier. "See What Undocumented Immigrants Carry Across the Border." *TIME Magazine*, 30 Jan, 2015, www.time.com/3647891/undocumented-immigrants-bags.

"Why are *The Economist*'s Writers Anonymous?" *The Economist*, 4 Sept. 2013, www.economist.com/blogs/economist-explains/2013/09/economist-explains-itself-1.

Other Sources

• **Blog**
Shaw, Julia. "The Memory Illusion." *Mind Guest Blog*, Scientific American Blogs, 13 June 2016, blogs.scientificamerican.com/mind-guest-blog/the-memory-illusion.

• **Comment on a forum**
Elle. "Charlotte Bronte: A Fiery Heart." *So Many Books*, 6 Apr. 2016, 3:10 a.m., somanybooksblog.com/2016/04/05/charlotte-bronte-a-fiery-heart.

• **Email**
Smith, Jane. "Re: The Tempest and Female Figures." Received by John J. Smith, 12 Mar. 2013.

• **Film or movie**
Mean Streets. Directed by Martin Scorsese, performance by Robert DeNiro and Harvey Keitel, Warner Brothers., 1973.

• **Same film or movie with a focus on DVD features**
Mean Streets. 1973. Directed by Martin Scorsese, performance by Robert DeNiro and Harvey Keitel, Warner Brothers, 2004, disc 5.

• **Letter**
Melville, Herman. "Letter to Nathaniel Hawthorne." *Hawthorne Paper Collection*, University of New Hampshire Library, 6 Aug. 1850.

• **Musical score**
Williams, John. Hedwig's Theme. Warner Brother's, 2005.

• **Oral presentation**
Alkalimat, Abdul. "eBlack: Revolution in the Revolution." Digital Diasporas Conference, 2 May 2008, University of Maryland, College Park.

• **Performance**
Our Town. By Thornton Wilder, directed by John Smith, performed by Philip Fitzgerald and Lana King, Amateur Theatre Company, 15 January 2014, Buell Theater, Denver.

• **Personal interview**
Smith, Stephen. Personal interview. 5 Nov. 2002.

• **Print interview**
Dreifus, Claudia. "A Conversation with Ellen Bialystok." *New York Times*, New York ed., 31 May 2011, p. D2.

• **Same interview, online**
Dreifus, Claudia. "The Bilingual Advantage." *New York Times*, 31 May 2011, www.nytimes.com/2011/05/31/science/31conversation.html

• **Sound recording**
Foo Fighters. *In Your Honor*. RCA, 2005.

• **Television or radio**
"Bass Player Wanted." Narrated by Bob Saget, directed by Pamela Fryman, *How I Met Your Mother*, CBS, 16 Dec. 2013.

• **Television or radio with a focus on individual contributions**
Pelosi, Nancy, performer. "Paulson, Pelosi & Ayahuasca." *Chelsea*, season 1, episode 19, *Netflix*, 23 June, 2016, www.netflix.com/title/80049872

• **Tweet**
Author. "Full text in place of title." Publisher, publication date and time, location.

@Zen_Moments. "I'm not afraid of storms, for I'm learning how to sail my ship. ~ Louisa May Alcott." *Twitter*, 24 June 2016, 1:48 p.m., twitter.com/Zen_Moments/status/746444977572614144

• **Visual art**
Leonardo da Vinci. *Mona Lisa*. 1503–1506? Oil on poplar. The Louvre, Paris.

• **Website**
Smith, Martha Nell, *et al.*, editors. *Dickinson Electronic Archives*. University of Maryland, 1994, www.emilydickinson.org/index.html

U.S. $7.95
Author: Kaitlyn McNamee/ Elizabeth Ronne

Find us on Facebook

6 54614 04834 9

hundreds of titles at **quickstudy.com**

ISBN-13: 978-1423248347
ISBN-10: 1423248341

50795
9 781423 248347